He Can Move Mountains;
Stop Holding Them in Place.

Angie I pray God blesses you more than you can Imagine!!

Love Always,

Tammie Lee

9103303251

tammieleeministries@gmail.com

He Can Move Mountains; Stop Holding Them in Place.

Tammie Lee

XULON PRESS

Xulon Press
2301 Lucien Way #415
Maitland, FL 32751
407.339.4217
www.xulonpress.com

Paperback ISBN-13: 978-1-6628-3535-3
Ebook ISBN-13: 978-1-6628-3617-6

Dedication

This book is dedicated to the ones that feel unloved and loved. The ones that struggle with insecurities and have strength. This is for the ones that want to undo what they can't and be who God says they are.

Jessica, I said you have a story that would help transform others one day. God will see to it that it does. This book is for all the battles that have been lost and won.

Irrevocably, I dedicate this to the ones I love deeply, my husband Antoine, my Children and their spouses, my Grandchildren, and my MOM! For, without them, I would not have the journey I have.

In loving memory, Kev and Jess... until we meet again, your love will go on touching the lives of others!

Acknowledgment

Mainly, I would like to give gratitude to The Father, Son, and Holy Spirit for assisting me with the inspiration and peace to write this book.

To all my Pastors, you have taught me the word of God to be accurate and unshakable. You have each shown me the sincerest form of grace. It has been an honor to have you in my life and serve God with you.

To Rhonda, who has never stopped believing in me, you've prayed and encouraged me for two decades to do God's assignment. I would not be in this place today without your steadfastness. You are more to the world than you will ever know!

To Irene, who taught me in the power of revelation knowledge, you've inspired me to trust the guidance and discernment of the Holy Spirit within me. Your reinsurance has helped me step into my calling. You're my confidant and always will be!

I would also like to acknowledge the wonderful people that have stood beside me in my good times and bad. To the ones that have walked quietly behind the scenes. To the ones that only want to be shown love. I appreciate you, Renee, Janie, Crystal, Sherry, Christine, Christie, Terri, Heidi, and ALL with whom I've encountered growth and/or support.

Mom, thank you for loving me the way you knew and letting God heal our hearts. May you continue your walk with him until it is time to go home! Love You Eternally!

Introduction

No one is immune to difficulties. We all have struggles. We don't grow being airlifted to the summit of the mountain. We grow when we climb that mountain with the weight of the world around us, while God says we don't have to carry those burdens as we climb. He is at the summit of the mountain, and we are guided with His strength. We climb and climb, thinking that's what we're supposed to do while sweat and tears drop from our sweet faces. We scream out repeatedly, and God sits waiting on us, and we ignore Him as though we don't see Him. Let Him, with all of His strength, pull you to the summit.

Stop allowing the things that cause you to stress to burden you down. God is the only mountain to remain. He is the Apex, the Alpha and Omega, the First and Last! He can move your mountain if you stop holding it in place. Your mountain is nothing more than a gift that assists in growing you into the ultimate Christian.

Your place in Christ is a journey with a final destination. You'll never heal if you never acknowledge hurt. I pray my testimony within this twelve-week Bible study helps you see the potential God has put inside you.

Just because life isn't turning out the way you want doesn't mean life isn't turning out exactly how it's supposed to. Don't be discouraged by where you are today, be encouraged by where you are going!

Table of Contents

WEEK 1

Be Careful Wanting to Revisit Your Past

On October 12, 2019, we were in the car driving in town when we came upon this roadblock that stopped us. The sky was cloudy with a haze in the air. It felt so muggy and hot. We could not go on with our journey for the day. There were military soldiers, and they had a training exercise. They were firing back and forth, preparing for battle.

As we watched them, as they trained, loud bombs were going off. We would have to cover our ears at times because it was so intense. Suddenly, one of the military soldiers was injured. Not only was he injured, but he died. As I watched this event happen, it was devastating. I ran to the solder and began to weep. I felt as if my child had died. I had thoughts of sorrow, wondering how the family would handle the death of their child. I can't even explain what the Lord had shown me to the level I experienced it. When I woke up, I was relieved it was only a dream.

That morning, the Lord expressed many of us don't even make it past the training to go into the actual battle. We grow weary during that time, and we give up, and that's not even the battle. We have to understand the training is intense for a reason. It drives us so that we make it live out of the struggle and do what He's called us to do for His Kingdom.

We cannot lead others if we are not filled with strength, endurance, planning, focus, direction, etc. Everything that makes a good soldier in Christ is done during training. May we all become strong disciples so that when we go into the battlefield, we will win others to Christ and teach them to be more outstanding disciples than we are. Every generation needs to be stronger than the next, for every generation will be more challenging than the last.

October 13, 2019, started just like any other Sunday. I was getting ready for church and called my daughter Jessica, only she didn't answer the phone. We knew that that wasn't unusual for Jessica. I figured she and the kids were still asleep, and she would call me later in the day. We went about our day, and I knew she would have family pictures done that evening, so I thought I'd hear from her close to that time.

That evening we went out to a piece of land that we had recently contracted with my son and daughter-in-law. We were so excited to show them what God was doing, and then it all came to a halting screech. It will be embedded in my brain forever.

My daughter-in-law answered her phone and screamed out, what do you mean Jessica's dead?! I fell to my knees. No mother should ever receive that phone call. We rushed in the car, drove as fast as possible to get to Jessica's home, only to be met by my oldest son. He just shook his head and said, "You can't go in there." Once again, I fell to my knees, screamed, and mourned for my daughter. All I could remember was my grandchildren walking around, confused by everyone's behaviors.

One by one, family members arrived. Everyone stayed in the driveway, trying to comfort each other the best they could. I could not get myself together. I was dying inside. They called the ambulance because they thought I might be having a heart attack. EMT whisked me away in the ambulance; it was all a blur. I cannot be living this nightmare again. Four years prior, my husband had died of a massive heart attack. I felt like this couldn't be real! I was starting to heal from the loss of my husband that I had been with for twenty-three years.

What had I done to deserve this? Why was Satan after me? Why was this happening again? Lord, I prayed for you to deliver her, to set her free from the demons that haunted her. "Why Lord, why?" So much pain, so many questions, so much uncertainty, and no vision of how this could turn out good. I wasn't sure what to do. I remember lying in the hospital bed where numerous friends and family would come in to check on me one by one. Still in shock, the only thing I knew was as I walked out this process, I would pull from the depths of my soul the Holy Spirit and would be able to handle it. I could hear my Father in heaven saying, "They're all watching you, Tammie, and how you respond will cause many of them to have the strength to keep going or a loss of belief in me."

When Kevin, my deceased husband, passed, I did not grieve very well. I was leaning on my own emotion and understanding. After I went through that journey, I told the Lord that I would need Him to be my strength 100 percent if I ever had to endure that pain again. I would not be able to do it alone. I wanted people to see God's glory in everything in my life, especially in the cruelest of moments.

> *'Likewise the Spirit also helps in our weaknesses. For we do not know what we should pray for as we ought, but the Spirit Himself makes intercession for us with groanings which cannot be uttered. Now He who searches the hearts knows what the mind of the Spirit is, because He makes intercession for the saints according to the will of God.' — Romans 8:26-27 NKJV*

I wanted to honor my Father and not break in my weakness. I'm not saying that anyone needs to grieve like anyone else. It is an individual journey, whether it is divorce, death, friend, loss of a job, home, or anything else you feel has been taken from you. You have a right to grieve in any way that helps you. However, never forget your Father is the comforter of your soul if you let Him. People are watching, and they want you to win the battle, so they have hope for their journey.

Let's talk about Jessica for a moment. She was the most free-spirited child I had. She never met a stranger and was very helpful as well as concerned about others. Jessica was a fantastic soccer player. She was a hard worker, beautiful, a tremendous mother, strong-willed, driven, a warrior, independent, intelligent, a student, and the list could go on.

What was so distinct about Jessica is she loved God very much in her unique way! Unfortunately, Jessica battled the demon of mental illness and drug addiction. She would excel at times then at other times struggle. As a parent, you carry your child's pain and their successes. You want to repair items in their life that need fixing and celebrate all their triumphs.

I realized when she passed away that I could never have saved her. I thought if I did everything a certain way, it would turn out whole for her. I was wrong. We cannot change the outcome of someone's life. It is a personal journey that they have to walk alone. What we can do is pray, encourage, and love them along the way! In the end, it is their walk. One with mirrors that show the depths of their soul. One with sounds of grievances of their past. One with fast rushing waters of their journeys of good and evil. Moments where time stands still.

The ones that we know of, the ones that hold us in our chains. Many times, our mountains are too high to climb and our valleys are too deep. You know the ones I am speaking of, which make us believe the lies of the enemy. The ones that say it is too late, we are not enough; it is the life sentence of our minds. Jess had that battleground and could not keep it a bay.

Despite this, God knew her time was near, and He spoke to me and said, invite your daughters and daughters-in-law to church for the lady's meeting. I thought, "Lord, there is no way I will be able to get them all together." God said, "No, Tammie, you will not, but my Spirit will." So, I purchased six tickets. God is perfect because that conference was two weeks before Jess's passing. On the night of the conference, she rededicated her life to Christ. I could rest knowing she was saved.

Jess always knew her life was going to be fast. She would constantly say, "I feel like there is not enough time to get done everything I need to complete." Jess was only two classes from her associate's degree and her dream to be a social worker. She wanted to support others, just as she had been supported so many times in her past. However, she could not leave her past to be presented with her future. Don't stop to look back in the mirror. It is a reflection that can get you trapped.

She continued to let the people in her life that did not have good intentions for her. The word of God says to guard your heart, and there is a reason for that. Jesus did walk with the sinners of this world, as He was about His Father's business, not His own. Once you have the strength the defeat your demons, then, and only then, do you have the power to fight for others. Loving others at a distance doesn't make you "better than them," it makes you aware of your possible weakness. He wants what is best for all of His people. He will take care of them.

Let God seek out the best council for them. You rest in his promise for you and let his Spirit work out the world. When it is time, He will reveal you to the world. God may need to hide you for a season. Just like He did, Jesus, let go and let God repair what the world has done to you. Let His holy spirit minister to you and give Him time to do His work. He has great plans for your life. Don't be in a hurry to get ahead of Him. Timing is everything!

It was many months later before we knew her cause of death. Everyone was shocked, even the coroner. She revisited her past, and it cost Jessica her life. But in that moment of death at Jess's celebration of life, people were saved.

> *'Likewise, I say to you, there is joy in the presence of the angels of God over one sinner who repents.'" — Luke 15:10 NKJV*

God's word says He will turn everything to good, EVERYTHING. There are moments when you want to lose hope because you are at a loss for helping but don't. God is waiting and watching. He has excellent plans. Even when you don't see Him working, He is. Now, to man, it looks like Satan won in the end. No, God won!

Satan may have brought her demon to visit her, but God brought His Spirit to save her. You see, although Jessica had a small beginning, over fifteen people received salvation at her celebration. To many, it was a small beginning. To God, there was joy in the presence of the angels. Never regret small beginnings.

> *'For who has despised the day of small things? For these seven rejoice to see The plumb line in the hand of Zerubbabel. They are the eyes of the Lord , Which scan to and fro throughout the whole earth.'" Zechariah 4:10 NKJV*

DATE: ____________________

Are you Struggling with revisiting your past?

____

What about your past keeps a hold on you?

____

____

____

____

____

____

Do you believe God can deliver you and if so, how?

____

____

____

____

____

____

Discussion Notes, Thoughts, Prayers, and Additional Scriptures:

Discussion Notes, Thoughts, Prayers, and Additional Scriptures:

WEEK 2

Do Not Let Your Past Define You

As you transition on your journey, I pray you are clothed in His righteousness. Don't be moved by what you think you cannot accomplish. There are so many times in our lives we put ourselves in boxes because of our past. What can I possibly do for you, God? Look at me. I am a complete mess. No, you are not a complete mess; you are a work in progress. God is always working on you. When you are in the middle of your biggest struggles, the most significant artwork is being designed. It will not define who you are. It will explain where you have been.

God has a different work for us all to create in this thing called life. Each of us has a calling, and don't try to fit into someone else's walk because it wasn't designed for you. It was intended for them. At the same time, don't think your calling isn't just as important as theirs. Focus on what you see God is doing in your life. The creator is waiting on you. You are not waiting on the creator. Your design has already been inspired. It is time for you to paint the picture for the rest of the world to see. Although we must be aware of our sin, we cannot let it hold us back. Walk it out! Make way for it not to define you but develop you.

Have you ever stopped to look at someone and noticed a void in their eyes? That void is their loss of hope. In our lifetime, there will be times when we see ourselves through the eyes of others. You should be careful who you are looking at because they can define you in their opinions and not in God's.

People are just that, people. Some have good intentions and some not so good, but if you wait for a man's approval, you'll be waiting a very long time. It was once said that once a person forms an opinion about someone, it is tough to change it. There is great truth in that statement. The sorrow that lies in it is that it keeps you exactly where man believes you belong.

But God, well, God is different. He doesn't see us where we were or even where we are. He sees us where we are going. Do not get trapped in the cycle of approval. When you decide that is where you belong, you trap yourself. Notice I said YOU. That is because our God is one of redemption! He wants us to have salvation and success. God believes in His creation so much that He sent angels to protect us from ourselves. See, we were designed for His pleasure, and with that, He wants us to grow just like we love watching those around us grow.

> *"'You are worthy, O Lord, To receive glory and honor and power; For You created all things, And by Your will they exist and were created.'" — Revelation 4:11 NKJV*

Because of this, God knew the path you were going to walk out. He desired so much for you, but in the end He knows what you will do; the good, bad, ugly, wonderful, beautiful, everything. He knew we would sin, not some, all.

No one is above sin. No one. Do not shame yourself for where you have been. That is not God's design. He knew it would happen before it did. What He desires is true repentance. For some of us, it is quick and not as difficult. For others, it is extremely hard. Neither is greater than the other. It has the power to break what is holding us. There are times when it takes us longer to break from the shame that binds us because we cannot forgive ourselves.

> *'for all have sinned and fall short of the glory of God, ' — Romans 3:23 NKJV*

God is right here, waiting. As you read this chapter, breath in God's forgiveness for you. Remember, you are not what you have done. You are what God has designed you to be. Ask Him to show you that. Ask Him to give you visions and dreams of what He has for you. Don't let your sin design you! If you have not already received Christ as your savior, take the time now.

Father, for those that have received salvation in the past, may they renew their mind at this very moment to receive all you have for them. For those who are just beginning to find you and their relationship with you, may they have the freedom that is accessible to each of us and come to know your son, Jesus. That they would know he died for their sins so they would repent and receive forgiveness. May they repent of anything keeping them from knowing you. I pray they ask for complete forgiveness and healing of their heart. In Jesus Name, Amen!

> *'The Lord is my light and my salvation; Whom shall I fear? The Lord is the strength of my life; Of whom shall I be afraid?' — Psalms 27:1 NKJV*

God wants you to walk out of your journey with love and faith and lean on him for guidance. Your life is full of tests, trials, and triumphs, just like the Bible. We always want to know the story's end. We all want God to lay it out. "Just tell me what is going to happen next, Lord."

I had made so many mistakes in my life. If it didn't look good, then I would have a reason to quit. On the flip side, if it looked good, I could show my face again. That is not how God does it at all. We have to face our past to be able to move into our future. Now we don't stay in it, but we have to acknowledge it. Acknowledging our sins and pain takes time. No one wants to look at what we look like internally.

On top of that, everyone wants to rate sin. Murder has a level. If you have an affair, another level. If you steal, level there too. Then, if you judge, lie, gossip, well, more levels. Truth is with God there are no levels. It is all the same to our Father.

For two years, I re-lived thirty years over and over. The Holy Spirit came to be with me during that time. He had to comfort me through that journey. You see, I had done some regrettable things in my twenties that weren't very pleasant to many people, primarily to my Father in heaven. I grieved in a way that was so difficult and painful. I was not the person I looked like on the surface. I was a little girl trapped in a woman's body that made decisions based on my life experiences. How many of us do that? Everyone does. It is what forms us into whom we become.

For me, the lies the enemy told me were very painful, too painful even to discuss. I didn't want to be judged by others because the judgment I placed on myself was enough. Fortunately, sin can only be hidden for a season. The saddest part is it usually reveals itself to the people closest to the sin. Whatever the reason, anything done in the darkness will always be shown in the light. One day we have to answer for what we have done. The greatness of the Father is he does it for conviction, not condemnation. A man may have other plans, but God is unchanging.

When I was small, I had been sexually abused numerously for many years by different people in my life. Since my mom and I had a very distant relationship, I could not tell her what was happening. Partly was because I was young and afraid. Then, as I was older, it involved shame. It was bad enough my biological father left my mother and me before I even knew him well. On top of that, my brother had passed away at fourteen days old from SIDS when I was four. She had enough on her shoulders.

I always told myself he did not want to leave me and could not handle my brother's death. Truth is, he wasn't there anyway. During my younger years, I had a very divided life from my mother and father's family. I don't want to give

Satan glory. However, I want you to know when unpleasant events happen to people, they look at themselves differently. Everyone takes unnecessary destruction and handles it in different ways. For me, I saw what seemed to be my value in all the events that occurred to me. That Spirit enslaved me until the day I decided I would no longer be in bondage to it.

I was more than that; I was a woman of God. That was when I was able to birth my elephant. What I mean by that is the birthing of elephants is close to a two-year process. Can you imagine being pregnant for almost two years? During those two years, God showed me I would learn who I was and why I made those decisions in my early years. Not for him to condemn me but for Him to raise me.

I had to confront all the facets of my life and let the Holy Spirit guide me out of the condemnation man and the enemy had set for me. Don't get me wrong, Satan still raises his head from time to time to remind me of what he says I am not. I speak the word of God and say, "Get behind me, Satan." Then, I remind him of who I am.

You see, we can be manipulated by Satan very easily. If you don't believe me, think about this for a moment. The unforgiving heart, the anger, the jealousy, the offense you may have for others or yourself, the devil sees it. Satan has you where he wants you in those moments. Only when we release forgiveness towards ourselves and others can we move forward. Don't be distracted. These times do not define you. God defines you.

> *'But those who wait on the Lord Shall renew their strength; They shall mount up with wings like eagles, They shall run and not be weary, They shall walk and not faint.'* — *Isaiah 40:31 NKJV*

DATE: ______________________________

Does your past define you?

____

Do the opinions of others stop you from doing what God has called you to?

____

____

____

____

____

____

Have the thoughts of your pain and judgments left you in a place of condemnation?

____

____

____

____

____

Discussion Notes, Thoughts, Prayers, and Additional Scriptures:

Discussion Notes, Thoughts, Prayers, and Additional Scriptures:

WEEK 3

Actions Occur Before Manifestations

'But without faith it is impossible to please Him, for he who comes to God must believe that He is, and that He is a rewarder of those who diligently seek Him.' — Hebrews 11:6 NKJV

When my children were small, we were a soccer family. When I say soccer, we would eat, breathe, and sleep it. We were at the fields seven days a week and would play anywhere from three to eight soccer games on the weekends. Those were some of the most incredible times of our children's lives. We would coach their teams to know one of us would be at most of the games. People always said if we kept our children active, they would stay out of trouble. There's a lot of truth in that statement.

However, I believe what keeps children out of trouble is keeping them balanced. For us, we lacked in that area during those years. I guess you could say we were an all or none type of family. Our children were deeply engaged in soccer, and we found very little time for our spiritual growth in the church for that season in our life.

We would do like most busy families. When we had an event for church to attend, we would develop reasons we couldn't get there. It was a small, subtle step as we drifted away from what we knew we needed. You see, that's how the devil works. It's one day here and one day there. Before you know it, you're entirely out of fellowship.

Then, the day came when we realized it was apparent, we were out of balance. We never even realized it happened because our family was so close during those soccer years. We had something that brought us together and made us feel connected. The truth is people like coming together with opportunities that unite them. Whether it's a sports arena, a club of some sort, church, anything that brings people together with a level of camaraderie makes us feel good. That is the reason the Kingdom is designed that way. God's design is we have unity.

When we're in those places, it disguises itself in a familiar way to us. The problem is it's not God's ultimate design. It's only part of it. I'm not saying you should not have extra activities in your life. I'm saying to be transparent and honest with yourself. Make sure God is first.

Right now, would you say you are in balance with God? Is He first and everything else second? Do you have a passion for God like you have a passion for other things? Are you sharing the life of God with people in the events of your life, or are you ashamed to share your beliefs?

During that time, God reminded me I needed to show a greater appreciation for the walk he had given me. I suppose you could say it was the moment that brought me back to my faith. My daughter Jess was at soccer practice when she suddenly started having an exercise-induced asthma attack.

What made this time so scary compared to other moments was we didn't have her inhaler. As she began struggling to breathe, I ran out to her! My heart just sunk! I thought, "What am I going to do now!" It was one of those moments, as though I couldn't even get my thoughts about myself. You know the moment where you're looking in your child's face, and you feel so helpless? But then Jess said, "Mom, start praying tongues!"

I had just spent two years in great repentance for a time of sin in my life where I was so ashamed. Who am I to speak with boldness, who am I to pray publicly, who am I to stand on the Open soccer field with everyone watching and declare the power of the Holy Spirit? Who am I? The thoughts were endless in my head, even though it had only been a matter of seconds. Then Jess yelled again, "Mom, PRAY in tongues." There we were, standing in the middle of the soccer field. My baby had enough knowledge and faith to know only God could help her.

With everything I had inside me, including all of my brokenness, I yelled out to my Abba Father! I prayed with an act of Faith that was no longer concerned with what people would say or what they thought of me. My daughter needed a miracle, and I was not going to be restrained. At that very moment, she took a deep breath, and then it happened, God's breath of life. That day broke me. It showed me no matter where I had been, ashamed of God was not one of them.

> *So Jesus said to them, "Because of your unbelief; for assuredly, I say to you, if you have faith as a mustard seed, you will say to this mountain, 'Move from here to there,' and it will move; and nothing will be impossible for you." — Matthew 17:20 NKJV*

I knew I had to have actions of Faith before I could have any God manifestations. I could not be concerned with what my past looked like because that would stop me from moving into God's future. I knew I needed to move forward and do what God had called me to do. Otherwise, I would have stayed in our place of shame forever. Neither man nor the enemy had the power to keep me from moving forward.

Since I was saved, believed Jesus Christ as my Lord and Savior, forgiven of all my sins, and God said He could turn everything together for good for those that love Him, then why would I stay in the place of condemnation? I had to trust God to meet my needs. I had to believe in the power of prayer! I accepted the Lord was my shepherd, and I believed he laid down His life for me, and He knew every need I had.

There it was, the moment that changed my life from sin and shame to love and Liberty. God never leaves us. His Holy Spirit is always with us. He stays with us even when we disappoint Him! We are struggling with our sin season because of our guilt and condemnation. In that, God never changes. He forgives you in your darkest moment. This is the time when you can make a permanent decision in a temporary situation.

Don't stop praying because you feel shame. Pray through it. Don't stop reading the word because you think you're unqualified. Read through it. Don't stop worshiping God because you do not feel worthy. Worship as though

He is sitting in the room with you. God has so many perfect attributes, don't let your sin find a way to make you less deserving of God's love. God is working on us one day at a time, one flesh at a time, one mind at a time.

> *'Not that we are sufficient of ourselves to think of anything as being from ourselves, but our sufficiency is from God, ' — II Corinthians 3:5 NKJV*

During this season of great work, remember, God is working on all of us. Some of us just take a little bit longer to be reformed. Again, actions of faith lead to the manifestations of God. Do it with fear and while trembling, believing God is a God of restoration.

DATE: ______________________________

Are you in balance with God?

____

What may keep you from being public about your faith?

____

____

____

____

____

____

How can you help others move forward from feeling condemned for their past?

____

____

____

____

____

____

Discussion Notes, Thoughts, Prayers, and Additional Scriptures:

Discussion Notes, Thoughts, Prayers, and Additional Scriptures:

WEEK 4

To Take a Drink or Not

When I was three years old, I had woke up earlier than my mom and dad. Just like any kid, you wake up hungry and thirsty. This particular day was like no other. My parents had a few friends over and spent the evening drinking.

I trotted my little self down the hallway and saw a big glass of orange juice sitting on the counter. I decided to get it down and drink it. When my mom got up, she started vacuuming and noticed I was falling over the vacuum and into things. So, she looks over and realizes the large cup of orange juice was empty. I didn't know the glass of orange juice was made up of half vodka.

Now, my mom didn't make a big fuss about it, unlike me as a parent. I would have freaked out. Back then, things were done differently. The bottom line is neither here nor there. How often do we drink something we shouldn't because people influence us to put things in our bodies that are not safe? How often have you been offered things that looked refreshing? Then, afterward, it ended up being detrimental to you? The same goes for our minds. How many times have we allowed something in our mind because it felt good? Then, it destroyed us from the inside out.

Be extremely careful when you start looking around and deciding what is best for you. We are to protect ourselves from our thoughts and actions. We are also to protect ourselves from the influences of others. God says we are to know His word.

> *'For whatever things were written before were written for our learning, that we through the patience and comfort of the Scriptures might have hope. ' — Romans 15:4 NKJV*

It's our job to be in the word as much as our pastors, teachers, mentors, friends, colleagues, etc. Although it may be their job to bring the word to us and encourage or uplift us, it is our job to study the word too. If you question what someone is saying, look it up. The word is the same yesterday, today, and tomorrow.

'Jesus Christ is the same yesterday, today, and forever. ' — Hebrews 13:8 NKJV

There are so many toxins and misrepresentations of God's word in the world, or as I like to call them, chameleons. Things of the world like to mimic the word of God so it can suck you into the abyss. It doesn't have a solid foundation. It is running on emotion and intellect. When the Lord teaches you His word, you are trained with Revelation knowledge. Meaning you cannot have the knowledge God has without Him revealing it to you.

You can read the Bible from back to front every year, yet it is only when God decides you will have a complete understanding you will have it. That is why God keeps us on milk and then gives us meat when we're ready, Hebrew 5:12-14.

You cannot compare God's word to the worldly institution of education and knowledge. God's thoughts are higher than ours. Therefore, our understanding is only when he makes it available. That is where the great debate between religion and spirituality comes in. I'm not going to get into that in this particular book. I am simply going to say be very conscientious of those that want to examine your knowledge in Christ. We are not to live in a place of debate with other Christians or even theologists, for that matter. We are all walking out of this journey with different steps.

Do not beat yourself up if you are not in a place where you know as much as the next person. However, always keep in mind that it is your responsibility to continue to grow in God's word. A journey between you and the Lord. Your fruits will speak for themselves, even if you do not have the knowledge someone else has.

I want to reflect on the first statement of my childhood I shared with you about orange juice. Because we are raising disciples in Christ, we must never forget they are taking a sip of what we are leaving out in the open for them to see. Keep in mind, we can offer our sin or our salvation as an example. This doesn't mean we're always going to have it together, but it does mean we're to be very aware of what our mere presence looks like to others. I speak from experience that I was not always the best steward of this.

> *'Therefore let us not judge one another anymore, but rather resolve this, not to put a stumbling block or a cause to fall in our brother's way.' — Romans 14:13 NKJV*

I struggled with even knowing what acceptable behavior as a Christian was. I finally came to a place in my life where

I had to sit back and let the Holy Spirit impress on me right from wrong. You don't know what you don't know. Some people were fortunate enough to have guidance in those areas. I was on the other end of the spectrum. I was not taught Bible protocol. I had to learn that as I became an adult and my frontal lobe developed a touch more. I was, what I like to call, a late bloomer. Everyone has giftings from God, and sometimes that gifting doesn't quite align with your calling yet because you haven't honed in your understanding of God. Take your time, don't beat yourself up, and know we are all a work in progress.

I mention all this to you because we tend to find our value in the directions that others lead us. Some of them leave a crumb sitting around for us to grab hold of, others give us information that may not be the best, some try to encourage us. In the end, it is our journey. The journey God has given us by His hand is the only journey. We will have multitudes of information presented to us throughout life. God shows us what to keep and what to dispose of, even what to hold for a later day. Do not be moved by how amazing someone speaks or even how poorly they do. Remember, God used who He deemed necessary for His Kingdom.

'But many who are first will be last, and the last first.' — Matthew 19:30 NKJV

You might not be the most articulate, poised, educated, or prosperous because you are a work in progress. God believes you are unique, and He loves you exactly where you are. So, again, ask yourself, "Should I take a drink or leave it?"

DATE: ____________________________

Have you taken a "drink" of something that you shouldn't have?

____

What influences you in areas of weakness?

____

____

____

____

____

____

What are some ways you can remove those hindrances?

____

____

____

____

____

____

Discussion Notes, Thoughts, Prayers, and Additional Scriptures:

Discussion Notes, Thoughts, Prayers, and Additional Scriptures:

WEEK 5

Love is a Variation for Man, Not for God

"Love" is the greatest commandment of all for God. We have heard this most of our life. Maybe it was phrased differently, but it is by far what the world wants us to focus on as well. Which is so unusual because that is not how they pursue it. The world teaches us tolerance, not love. They say without it, we would be a very selfish society. Yes, that is true … But the question is, "Is it love they are trying to manifest or tolerance?" You have to ask yourself, "Do we genuinely understand loves power with only a glimpse of that love?"

I have come to a place in my life where the revelation of love is so intense that, at times, it feels overwhelming. Think of times when you lost a loved one, been betrayed by a friend, lost a spouse to divorce, and so on. All of these bring grief, and it is from the love you have during those moments that you feel almost powerless. The hurt is overwhelming from the love that you held.

My mother once asked me when I realized she loved me. I said it was when I lost my husband. There was compassion that I never comprehended from God and His love of His creations until I lost someone that meant more to me than words could express. I even saw a love from my mother that I hadn't seen before.

I had a challenging childhood, not because my mother didn't love me, but because my mother only knew how to show the love she knew. Love is a variation of ways for everyone in human form. You can only offer your understanding of love. Don't discount someone's act of love if it's the only way they know how to express it.

The Bible tells us what God sees love as, and it is evident. However, when someone does not know what that looks like, they do their best, not God's. Then you have to ask yourself, what is my place in this love? Do I resent them or forgive them? Do I retaliate or release? Do I confirm or deny? What standard does God expect from us in return? As you engage yourself in my journey, please know that yours may look quite different, but, in the end, it all boils down to one main component, love.

When I was married to my deceased husband, we would retaliate so often that our love would grow cold to one another continually. Each of us had our own demons to battle. Still, instead of remembering we fight against principalities and not flesh and blood, we would try and destroy each other from the depth of our wounds.

Love is the most powerful weapon all people own. Although we loved each other, we could not keep ourselves from destroying the main gift that God had given us, LOVE. It was through His death that I finally understood love on a whole new level. The level God wants us all to know it on.

> *'Love suffers long and is kind; love does not envy; love does not parade itself, is not puffed up; does not behave rudely, does not seek its own, is not provoked, thinks no evil; does not rejoice in iniquity, but rejoices in the truth; bears all things, believes all things, hopes all things, endures all things. Love never fails. But whether there are prophecies, they will fail; whether there are tongues, they will cease; whether there is knowledge, it will vanish away. ' — I Corinthians 13:4-8 NKJV*

Understand this scripture is the finale of love. Don't be discouraged if you can't see yourself or others in this light because I can assure you, we all have come short of this passage. There is not one of us that possesses all of these attributes. We are fleshly and human. However, the Spirit that is within each of us does. Therefore, we are capable. We have to yield to the Holy Spirit and remember our hearts begin to change as we grow in God. The most complex part of our journey is our responsibility to others. It is easy to stay loving when no one wrongs you and when you keep your circle small. But when you jump in the water with all the fish, it can be a tad more taxing. God does give us a great warning about guarding your heart.

> *'Keep your heart with all diligence, For out of it spring the issues of life.' — Proverbs 4:23 NKJV*

There is a great council with this warning… he knows a broken heart is hard to heal and can destroy the love surrounding it. No matter what you take from this book, I pray most that you take the love in which it was written.

> *'Though I speak with the tongues of men and of angels, but have not love, I have become*

> *sounding brass or a clanging cymbal. And though I have the gift of prophecy, and understand all mysteries and all knowledge, and though I have all faith, so that I could remove mountains, but have not love, I am nothing. And though I bestow all my goods to feed the poor, and though I give my body to be burned, but have not love, it profits me nothing.' — I Corinthians 13:1-3 NKJV*

Without love, we are empty. Standing when all else falls … with love, we can fight through. Many say that it is "little faith" that keeps us bound, but I disagree. I believe the lack of love is what keeps us bound. For, as our love grows, so does our faith. God is evident with instruction. We are very selective with hearing. I am not saying that faith is not an essential piece to God's direction, but I am saying that your faith means nothing to Him without love. You can preach any message you like about God's goodness, but if you can't love the one that tries to destroy you, you have accomplished nothing.

Love is exactly what caused my family to stand up and give a wonderful ending to my deceased husband's new beginning. As I wiped the tears from my face, my children would enter the place where I worked one by one. First, I directed those there to contact my oldest son, as I knew I would need his strength. Once he arrived, I gave him the sorrowful news. I will never forget the pain in his eyes and the unbelief that this was happening. Once I felt he was ready, I told him I would need him to step into the leadership role and help each child. I then allowed God to work.

One by One, they would enter the door, and we would love them through their moment. It was time to tell the last two of my sons. We met them at the house, and it was the most unspoken hurt that I couldn't even imagine. Although our pain was great, our Lord was greater. Friends and acquaintances showed up through the entire eight-day process to help with anything they could. Their love was amazing. I could not have asked for anything more during that week. You see, when people are hurting, people feel your pain. It's almost like God opens the darkest moment and allows His children to offer the most remarkable gift, love. I didn't know where everyone's walk was or where it was going, but I knew God was working at that very moment.

The following eight days were very intense for everyone. It took us some time to get Kevin's body back from the state he was located in. Thankfully, he worked for a fantastic company that took care of those expenses. They were simply sent from heaven! During that time, we had so many showing their love for our family in all aspects. It was the smallest of gestures that showed us God was with us. It is amazing how when someone passes, even those who don't know you, hurt with you. People find love deep within them and share it with you during times of grief.

It is hard to explain the pain you endure when you lose someone you love. He was my best friend since high school. Although our marriage was a very difficult one, our love was deep. So deep that no matter how many times we messed up, we never gave up. The way we would best describe it was "Beautiful Chaos" and "We functioned in our dysfunction."

Kevin had an incredible giving heart and loved the unloved. Sadly, he came from a tough background and had many demons that he couldn't contain. You see, my husband was in and out of work often because of the line of work he was in, construction. That realm of work was a very arduous and unsteady one. Regrettably, he was also a functioning alcoholic. Most Christians say sin is sin, yet the world has labeled it a disease. They are both right. It is a sinful disease, and only God can destroy it before it destroys you and the ones that love you. Although I did not battle what my husband did, I chose other sins. I had infidelity in the early years of our relationship. It's something I was extremely disappointed in myself over.

The most painful of all was I could not forgive myself, neither could others. It was when I was able to forgive myself, I was able to move on. God forgave me the moment I had true repentance. It was no longer about what others thought of me. It was what I looked like through my Father's eyes. I repented and gave it to God. I would love to say that it was over the moment I asked for forgiveness; it wasn't. It took years of reflection and me continually forgiving myself.

Kevin would hurt me so deep with his words and actions in the hard times, trying to break me. In turn, I would justify my behaviors. My hurt was consuming me because the man I loved could not love me the way I thought I needed to be loved. We were destroying each other! Many times, the only way to stop the pain between us was to say, "Let's get divorced." During those early years, I would always justify my behavior by, if he would, then I would or vice versa for him. A continual circle of hurt.

Then, a very astute man of God said, "If he had cancer would you leave his side?" That statement softened my heart to love him where he was. More importantly, it helped me start loving myself where I was. God knew my heart was broken, but He also knew I would be strong enough to make it through the valley.

I remember praying one afternoon for a colleague's marriage. When I finished, God said, "Now pray for your marriage the way you did for them." I could not believe what He was asking of me. Did he know what my husband had done to me? Had He seen the years of heartache? Had He seen the walls and items that had been broken? Yes, He saw it all! He saw all the damage and then some. He also saw what I did.

Deep in me, we all know why I didn't believe God would restore us. How could God heal something as broken as us? I had to wear a scarlet letter, and my husband wore many other letters. The beautiful thing about God is He is so unconditional that He loves us when we fall. The only true Agape love!

I prayed that day with all that I knew. I was laying it all down. I wasn't looking back. While praying, I had a vision of me taking my heart out. It was broken into two pieces. I then handed it to God. He closed his hands over my heart. You could see the glow of this beautiful light out from in between his fingers. There it was! My heart was now in one piece. I was never the same after that.

Although it wasn't a quick transformation for me to be a better wife and believer. It did happen over many years, with many mentors and millions of prayers. I had to change my assignment for my marriage. I didn't want tolerance for Kevin; I wanted unconditional love. The love that was not shaken by actions, the love that supported when the support looked broken, the love that understood hurt. I realized that although we were at different places, we were actually in the same place. Nonetheless, God healed us from that day forward and I am still being reformed with God's Love daily until this day.

As for Kevin, well, his battle was more complex. Over time, our life was softer, but it was still life. One with twists and turns, mountains and valleys. Best of all, it was ours. No explanations are needed. It may be a long journey to get their forgiveness for many, but we must remember that we are only accountable to God in the end, and He knows our hearts.

Six months before he passed, God had told me that he would be delivered of Alcoholism within six months, and he was. God does not always present the healing the way we want it, but He does heal the way they receive it. God knows each of us individually. Does God not know what our final destination looks like, the paths we will choose, or our desires? I was once told that we could change our direction just as God changes the wind. You see, we do have the will to do as we decide. The exception to that rule is if your treasure lies with the Lord, you will desire to please Him.

> *'For where your treasure is, there your heart will be also.' — Matthew 6:21 NKJV*

You'll begin to ask Him to help and pray without ceasing until He answers. Some demons are significant but never too big for God. We have to want it. You can't tell God you want to stop something and think a magical person will show up and take it away. It doesn't work like that; it is a heart change. You must reach into the depths of your soul.

He is right there speaking; all He is waiting for is your surrender. He wants to deliver you just as much as you want to be delivered, but there is a surrendering that must take place for Him to do what you are asking. During your life, continue to ask yourself, "Am I looking for tolerance or love?" Webster defines Tolerance as "**2a:** sympathy or indulgence for beliefs or practices differing from or conflicting with one's own." If you take time to ask God what we are to do in a time of great division, God's word is simple.

> *'Receive one who is weak in the faith, but not to disputes over doubtful things. For one believes he may eat all things, but he who is weak eats only vegetables. Let not him who*

eats despise him who does not eat, and let not him who does not eat judge him who eats; for God has received him. Who are you to judge another's servant? To his own master he stands or falls. Indeed, he will be made to stand, for God is able to make him stand.' — Romans 14:1-4 NKJV

DATE: ____________________________

Do you love someone or something more than God?

____

What can you do to redirect your hurt versus retaliation?

____

____

____

____

____

____

How can you help facilitate growth in your relationships?

____

____

____

____

____

____

Discussion Notes, Thoughts, Prayers, and Additional Scriptures:

Discussion Notes, Thoughts, Prayers, and Additional Scriptures:

WEEK 6

Life is Like a Pressure Cooker

In the world we live in today, the pressures of life seem like a pressure cooker. What it does is put so much intensity in our life that we forget about our calling. We get wrapped up in the moments, and they direct our paths instead of our path directing our moments. There you are, sitting at your desk, doing your work patiently. Suddenly, your boss sends you an email and demands that the situation get taken care of immediately.

There's an abundant amount of strategic placing in your world that has to occur for positions to be adjusted. In your boss's world, that's not their issue. Your boss knows a problem needs to be changed, and you have just been assigned the adjuster position. Now you start trying to take all the pieces and put them together. However, one part is just too much. You start getting frustrated, agitated, angry, and then you find yourself in a place of despair.

Then, everyone around you begins to be affected by the mere presence of your boss. Although they are not in direct contact with them. It spills over to home life since you can't get it off your mind, and your family is now affected by your boss that they have not had the pleasure of working with. As if that isn't enough, you have a few church services that you need to attend this week, and they get the enjoyment of your boss' presence as well. Now let me show you where we end. People can make our insecurities bigger than our calling! Your insecurity at that moment is that you're not going to achieve the outcome that your boss wants. Not because you're incapable of completing the task, but because many pieces have to come together to make that task attainable.

You're calling at any moment is to be Christlike. You hear so many times Christians say, "Find your purpose." Yes, there is a calling that you have been put on the earth to accomplish. Amid "the calling," you lose sight because of your frustrations and insecurities. All of us have insecurities. It's okay! It's okay to have insecurities. It's not okay to let them determine the path of your calling.

It stops us from completing our tasks. The tasks that are called to meet every day that we live on this Earth. We are called to make disciples by being Christlike. Now we all have variables of how that will be accomplished, but the ultimate goal is to develop disciples of Christ. Although I used an employer analogy, you can use this in all your situations. You have to take a moment where people put urgency on you and breathe.

In God's word, it says everything is to be done in decency and order. The more thoughts I have had on this, and the more times I've had to process this, I've realized the decency and order is also taking a moment to evaluate a situation and breathe. We cannot let the world direct our paths! God is designing you the way He wants. When the time is right, you'll know. In the meantime, do not let your insecurities put your puzzle together.

What's difficult about humans is we need to be appreciated. It doesn't matter who you are. Everyone wants to feel appreciated. Even a narcissist wants to feel appreciated. Though appreciation can only temporarily negate our insecurities. It doesn't eliminate it. It temporarily denies it.

In those moments, we are looking for the edification from man instead of the solid revelation from God. In essence, it affects our calling. We stop believing in who we are and how God made us. We start looking to people for validation when we don't feel appreciated.

I once heard it said if you feel valued, you'll do more than is expected. And the same goes for if you feel unappreciated, you'll do less than expected. The truth of the matter is whether people appreciate you or don't appreciate you, you're calling doesn't change. Callings aren't altered from sin in your past, how your boss views you, or whether a congregation accepts you. Callings aren't based on how you were treated as a child, or if people love you or lack thereof, they are not promoted or demoted by man. Your insecurities should never be more significant than you're calling. Don't let anyone's view about you determine your path!

> *'And that you put on the new man which was created according to God, in true righteousness and holiness. and be renewed in the spirit of your mind, that you put off, concerning your former conduct, the old man which grows corrupt according to the deceitful lusts,'*
> — *Ephesians 4:22-24 NKJV*

Spend time with the Father and let Him show you what He says about you. Let Him work on you from the inside out. Have you allowed the opinions of others to rent space in your head? Have you allowed their opinions to stop your calling? Maybe you just let the devil whisper in your ear and remind you of your past. It is okay to have emotion when these events occur temporarily. What is not okay is making decisions based on a provisional emotion.

> *'Casting down arguments and every high thing that exalts itself against the knowledge of God, bringing every thought into captivity to the obedience of Christ, ' — II Corinthians 10:5 NKJV*

For over seventeen years, I believed I was going to write books and speak. Even though in the midst of it, I thought I was unqualified. My life did not equate to what I believed God would require of me. Even people I surrounded myself with would only encourage a tiny piece of what I believed. Then, the Lord showed me that I must stay hidden until it was his timing to reveal me.

What I want you to take from that is, yes, sometimes people come out the gate running. For others, it may be a lengthy race. God's timing is perfect, and He knows precisely what he's doing in you and when He needs to reveal your fullness!

> *'To everything there is a season, A time for every purpose under heaven: A time to be*

> *born, And a time to die; A time to plant, And a time to pluck what is planted;' — Ecclesiastes 3:1-2 NKJV*

With God, there's no expiration date. We don't come with the instructions of "must be used by." If we have the qualified date to be born, we have the qualified date to be revealed. Even Jesus had to stay hidden for a short time. Don't look at your timeline and give up. There is no time limit.

Know that God is doing excellent work in you. Just as you would never put a time stamp on someone's salvation, please don't put one on your calling. God infuses you with everything He is, his entire presence, not part, all of Him. Never lose sight of what God has called you to do while you are in the pressure cooker.

DATE: ______________________________

Do you feel like you're in a pressure cooker?

____

What is everyday life keeping you from in your calling?

____

____

____

____

____

____

How can you adjust the pressure cooker to achieve what God has called you to?

____

____

____

____

____

____

Discussion Notes, Thoughts, Prayers, and Additional Scriptures:

Discussion Notes, Thoughts, Prayers, and Additional Scriptures:

WEEK 7

Unassuming

I was once having a conversation with a dear friend of mine. Someone that knew me when I was much younger and watched me evolve into the woman I am today. I made a brief comment I felt very naive to the world as a young girl. Her response was very thought-provoking. She said I was very unassuming. I wasn't quite sure of the whole meaning of that statement, so I looked it up. I found it interesting that Webster's dictionary describes it as, "Not having or showing any feelings of superiority, self-assertiveness, or showiness."

I am confident people who have met me in today's time would not necessarily share that enthusiasm. You see, the young girl in me has been designed by God and the world. Through the pain I endured, the testimony I share with you today was inspired by the Spirit of God. So many times people judge the book by its cover, but God wants us to look at His people through His eyes. This means we cannot make superficial judgments by the behaviors people have. We have to look deep within them and get to know them and understand their journeys. The Grace, our Father, shows us repeatedly is the Grace we should show others. Hurt people, hurt people. Sometimes unintentionally and truthfully, sometimes intentionally.

I was reminded of a few times in my life where my unassuming personality found me in a place of great controversy. The times when you unintentionally put yourself in compromising situations. Then they become compromising events. Then they become lifelong strongholds.

When I was younger, I hung out with some friends at an arcade locally in our town. It was a night like any other night. I had started getting the freedom I always wanted as a young teen. I started finding who I was as a person and rebelling against authority. I wanted to be cool and fit in with everyone else. I had some friends talking about getting some wine coolers. I was like yeah, let's find someone to help us. Be very careful about wanting what you want.

There was a guy that hung out there with all of us young teenagers. He was about early-mid-twenties. He said, "I'll run you down to the store to get some." I said, "Great, let's go." We got to the store. He went in to purchase the coolers, and he came back out to the car. As we drove back to the arcade, we took a minor side road unbeknownst to me. "What are we doing? Where are we going." He says, "You have to pay for the wine coolers." Unfortunately, this wasn't my first event, so I "paid." We then went back to the arcade as though nothing happened. I knew everyone would say it was my fault for putting myself in a situation like that, so I said nothing.

Since then, I have forgiven him. Most importantly, I forgave myself. Truthfully, I had no idea how to look at it because I was too young and, in my opinion, naive. I thought everyone behaved that way; it was an expectation that was set. I can't tell you who that guy was to this day.

'bless those who curse you, and pray for those who spitefully use you. ' — Luke 6:28 NKJV

Take a short journey with me. After that, I became promiscuous for a short time. I never really had value in myself or stood up for myself, even when I needed to. I was very reserved and put myself in situations that were very detrimental for me. Now journey a little farther to the age of twenty-seven. Everything changed, I realized I had a voice, and I could stand up for myself.

Regrettably, that was the polar opposite and the extreme side of my heart. I created a woman inside that externally was my protector. No one was going to sit me down, and no one was going to tell me what I could and couldn't do. I was going to stand up and fight for those that couldn't fight for themselves, as well as fight for myself. I was going to set the record straight, and it didn't matter what it looked like. What doesn't kill you makes you stronger.

No one was going to hurt me again. I was important, and if you didn't know, I would tell you. I was not going to let all of this hurt define me. Then I woke up and realized I had turned into the very things I hated. What had I done? Who had I become? My bitterness had blocked my heart from seeing the good. Now, with time, I've realized my assertiveness had to sit down on occasion. I did not have to defend who or what I was. I did not have to defend how others saw me. What I had to defend was that no one would be able to take advantage of me again.

It was going to take years to undo that unforgiveness. It was a process of wall after wall. I had to tear down the building I surrounded myself with and learn to love myself. Have you ever found yourself in a situation you felt you had to justify? Have you ever thought, "If you knew my side, you wouldn't look at me so bad?" Maybe you took the other extreme. Perhaps you decided you would say nothing, then people would continue to take advantage of you. Whether or not it was an opening we gave them or they just took it. Either way, we all have a right to be delivered from the pain caused by others and the pain we cause ourselves.

Don't believe you are defined by the hurts of your past. Know you have the power to determine your future. Keep in the front of your mind, the battle has already been won. The only way you stay strong is if you lean on the Father.

If I could go back in time and speak to that little fourteen-year-old girl, I would tell her you are enough! You don't have to fit in with the world! You are unique, and God has set you apart! You don't have to do anything that makes you feel less than loved!

> *'Trust in the Lord with all your heart, And lean not on your own understanding; ' — Proverbs 3:5 NKJV*

You may have put yourself in situations that are not the best, but be patient things tend to work out over time. Scars are only reminders of your strength, not your weakness.

DATE: ______________________________

Have you ever found yourself in a situation you felt you had to justify?

____

How can you take a difficult situation and turn it around for the Glory of God?

____

____

____

____

____

What event can you use to encourage others out of their trap?

____

____

____

____

____

Discussion Notes, Thoughts, Prayers, and Additional Scriptures:

Discussion Notes, Thoughts, Prayers, and Additional Scriptures:

WEEK 8

Are You Driftwood?

It was once said that life could be like Driftwood or a tree planted with deep roots. I often would ask myself which category would I fall into during different times of my life. We should all achieve a tree planted with deep roots. However, some only want to go as deep as Driftwood. For others of us, we start like Driftwood and then become trees planted with deep roots. I always keep in mind everything and everyone has a purpose in our lives. We may not always like what we see, but the results are good if we allow God to do good and perfect work inside of us.

> *'Make you complete in every good work to do His will, working in you what is well-pleasing in His sight, through Jesus Christ, to whom*

> *be glory forever and ever. Amen.' — Hebrews 13:21 NKJV*

When I was a small child, I came from a home with a faulty view of life. Sadly, my mother had a significant chemical imbalance in her brain that I wasn't aware of until my mid-twenties. She was an alcoholic and had been married eight times. Fortunately, I was only exposed to three. One of them was my stepdad that she was married to for over sixteen years. When I was twenty, my stepdad passed, and approximately one year later, so did my stepsister. It was such a difficult time for me. Mom engaged in additional relationships trying to find her way, leaving me with a deep void.

I tell you this not for you to judge my mother. I am telling you so you can have an image of what the enemy tried to use to set her up for failure. Even my extended family did not talk about it. Growing up, I thought everyone had a home like us.

Regrettably, my mother didn't want to take responsibility for her rebellious spirit or acknowledge her imbalance. She couldn't count the cost for herself or others around her. Her decisions were not because my mother was an evil person. Her imbalance and childhood were made for her. She did not wake up one day and decide to become an alcoholic or have a mental illness. It was a process that took years to unfold.

When I was younger, I didn't understand all of this. I took everything Mom did as a personal vendetta against me, a rejection of who I was. She once said to me, "How can I love others when I don't even know how to love myself?" In turn, it caused me to search out the things of the world that would make me feel loved.

I didn't understand what my mother meant; however, I completely understand now. My mother loved me to the ability of love that she had. I was just so young I didn't understand that concept. Although my mother did many things that weren't good for me, my mother also did things to the best of her ability.

Feeling unloved is an enormous trap of the enemy. God created us with one idea, to love. A perfect plan in an unperfect world. I would search out love in other ways. I was often getting myself into what I would call a dilemma. One that would eventually shape my life into what it is today.

I became a mother at a very young age. I was seventeen and a senior in high school when it happened. The unfortunate part was my mother wanted me to have an abortion. In her own way, she tried to protect me from making the same mistakes she did. However, I kept searching for something to fill the void I had throughout my life. I graduated high school with my eighth-month-old cheering from the stadium. I went on to be married and divorced shortly after that with two children. By twenty-four, I had three more children and was remarried. Never grasping the concept, I was just a child myself. Since I always believed children were a gift from God! My children made me feel loved and a connection to God.

I wanted the American dream! You know the spouse, children, house, pets, miniature stick people on the back window of the SUV. I was in such a rush to have everything I thought looked perfect, except I forgot one key component, healing. I should have taken time to work through some of the effects and the demons I battled as a child before I was ready to give what I didn't have to others. I am not saying we need perfection. I am just saying, if we are aware of our shortcomings, we may be more adaptable to work around them instead of others around us having to feel the negative consequences.

My mother and I had such a perplexing relationship. I could tell my mom wanted desperately to be the mom I needed. I could also tell my mother couldn't be the mom I needed. I never understood why my mom didn't push me to be a better person. She always let me settle for who I was. In that, there were mixed emotions. One was to be content with who you are. The other was, I should consistently achieve to be better.

I struggled with contentment. Truthfully, I didn't understand how to facilitate it. I wanted to be content, but I also had big dreams. The problem in that thought process is we should always try to achieve better. Otherwise, the world would remain stagnant. Always remain content with the concept of time. Waiting on God is that journey. I had many years where I didn't know how to achieve dreams and contentment. Then the Lord reminded me not to worry about tomorrow.

> *'But seek first the kingdom of God and His righteousness, and all these things shall be added to you. Therefore do not worry about tomorrow, for tomorrow will worry about its own things. Sufficient for the day is its own trouble.' — Matthew 6:33-34 NKJV*

There were always times when I said I wanted to be everything that my mother wasn't. As I sat and thought about my childhood, I realized I had it all wrong. There were aspects of my mother's life that I didn't need to have; they were unhealthy for me. There was a lot of love she had in her! Love that I would only come to understand as I got older.

Mom and I never really understood how to communicate. Say what you mean, and mean what you say didn't work for us. So instead of saying, "Tammie, you're too young to have a child. It will alter your life forever." She would say, "Maybe you should just have an abortion until you're ready." Before you start passing judgment, understand that my mother came from an environment that was acceptable behavior. When something didn't fit into your plan, you changed it. What my mother didn't understand was a baby was part of God's plan for me.

For a season, my children saved my life. They were the reason I woke up every morning, the reason that I thought I was worth something. I learned how to love through my children. They were the reason that I wanted to be a better me. Then there was that extraordinary moment when I realized that my children were not my reason. Jesus Christ was!

I realized my identity was not found in the lack of love I received, my mother, my love for my children, my successes in life, etc. My value came in the love of Jesus! My value came in the place that He opened up His arms and said, 'You are loved!' Maybe you're reading my book reflecting on your own journey, and you see your history being similar to mine. Ask yourself, "am I a reflection of my childhood? Am I a reflection of my spouse and children's love? Am I a reflection of all the achievements I've had in my life? Or am I a reflection of God's love!"

> *'I will praise You, for I am fearfully and wonderfully made; Marvelous are Your works, And that my soul knows very well.' — Psalms 139:14 NKJV*

Life has also taught me that my reflections may vary from one minute to the next. If I'm having a good day, I feel a little more connected to God. Then on the not-so-good days, I would have thoughts that God was so far away, and I was nothingness to Him. That is where it brought me back to seeing my life as Driftwood or a tree planted with deep roots.

When you think about Driftwood, it has its purposes. Driftwood can block water; it continues to fill up and provide necessary nutrients to wildlife. Plants can grow through Driftwood, giving them temporary stability. The tree that is planted with deep roots may never move. Driftwood left to itself will float until there's something to hold it in place. It stays firm and in place, providing shelter for many animals and nourishment, grounded to help others.

See, my mom was Driftwood. She would move about taking up a location to fulfill a need in her. Sprinkling a bit of this or that, never making deep connections. She thought as long as she produced what was expected, then that was an achievement. To some degree, it was, but it was never profound. It was just Driftwood. She would come and go as the current suggested. Unfortunately, I needed her to be my tree planted with the deepest roots, yet she couldn't do that.

Since then, God has repaired that time with roots that continue to flourish me into the tree that I needed from others. God has a way of taking all our hurts and planting us deep within Him. Maybe you are driftwood, maybe not. What I do know is our Father is capable of rooting us. Your circumstances do not determine your outcome. Drift or plant, it's up to you. Keep in mind blessed is the man who puts his trust in the Lord.

> "'Blessed is the man who trusts in the Lord , And whose hope is the Lord . For he shall be like a tree planted by the waters, Which spreads out its roots by the river, And will not fear when heat comes; But its leaf will be green, And will not be anxious in

the year of drought, Nor will cease from yielding fruit.' — Jeremiah 17:7-8 *NKJV*

DATE: ______________________

Are you Driftwood or a Tree with deep roots?

____

What can you do to grow yourself into a more profound person with God?

____

____

____

____

____

____

How can you build a sturdier root system to help others?

____

____

____

____

____

____

Discussion Notes, Thoughts, Prayers, and Additional Scriptures:

Discussion Notes, Thoughts, Prayers, and Additional Scriptures:

WEEK 9

One Word Changes a Whole Meaning

We have been blessed to go every year to the beach from the time I was a teen and stay a week at my mom's timeshare. That was the only vacation my family could go on for many years because my husband and I were not financially clever. Our children would look so forward to those few days at the beach. Their anticipation was always so great to watch. Those memories were some of the most fulfilling times in our life.

My husband, for the most part, would relax and enjoy our time there. We knew the stress would not come as often with us to the beach. Even in all the chaos, Kevin was such a great dad. He loved our children very much. I genuinely believe they kept him alive. He found his value in their success. Although Kevin had his problems, I always kept our children believing that he was the world's greatest dad, because he was! His demons were tremendous, yet his love for his children was superior. He would always love doing creative things with them when we went away. The condo always had classes and such for the kids and families to hang out and do. He would take at least one afternoon and do one with them. This particular year the association had a class on sea turtles.

My daughter Jess loved sea turtles. Truth be told, she loved anything that had to do with the ocean. I believe that it brought her peace. So, there they are, sitting in expectation for the information. At that time, my children ranged from nine years old to fifteen years old. The representative for the sea turtle program would educate them on everything. From how they protected them to why they were endangered and all in between.

Then, she made a statement about only having seven in the world. Jess very innocently looked over at her brother and said, "There are more than seven sea turtles in the world, right?" Everyone laughed and said, of course, there are. You see, if you miss one word, you miss the whole statement.

Isn't that very similar to our walk? Someone is telling you a story, and you miss a vital word, then the story means something very different. There are more than seven sea turtles in the world, and the word species was missing.

Maybe we only have parts of what God is showing us or even a fraction of what we need to do. That is why it is vital that you wait on God. For many of us, we want to rush God so that we can get to the finish line. Amid that haste, we miss what he is trusting us to do.

> *'And Jesus, answering them, began to say: "Take heed that no one deceives you. ' — Mark 13:5 NKJV*

Suppose God entrusts you with a ministry. You want to do it your way because you hear only part of the instruction. In that case, you could cause a downward trajectory. I am not saying do nothing. I am saying pause before you make assumptions or discord. Your intentions may be coming from a good place. Nevertheless, remember good places do not always represent God's places.

We think we have the right idea, and from time to time, God is saying something a bit different, only one word different, still different. You can see seven turtles, not seven million, and then there is God. He sees the seven million and then some. Take time to evaluate your path, take time to meditate on God's word, take time to know that you know.

> *'This Book of the Law shall not depart from your mouth, but you shall meditate in it day and night, that you may observe to do according to all that is written in it. For then you will make your way prosperous, and then you will have good success. ' — Joshua 1:8 NKJV*

I pray you will renew your strength in who you are during this journey, but mainly in who God is. The Great I am, Abba Father! He is your beginning and your end. He has so much for you in the middle if you unlock your mind to receive the revelation that God has for you.

Isn't life just like reading a book? Think about this for a moment. You like to anticipate the following sentence, the next chapter, the finale when you are reading. Right?! You want to ask God continually in life what happens next. You want the answers to everything. Maybe that is because you are scared, perhaps because you are hurt, discouraged, or you're excited, happy, nervous. Remember, if you rush through the story, you could miss critical points to the narrative.

I am confident that all of us have heard or read something and missed vital information. Is it fathomable that we may have just checked out for a minute or two? It could have been we were extremely busy, possibly uninterested in the moment. No matter the reason, the fact remains, it is easy to miss main details that can derail us from our destiny.

Until this day, we all still giggle when we think of Jess and those seven sea turtles. However, more important than the joy she brought to us, she brought us life lessons that will go on for eternity. Lessons, such as taking time and listening to those around you because it may be the last time you hear their voice and, in the midst, realize one word can make the difference in their story and yours.

DATE: ______________________

Have you ever had a situation where you only heard part of the story?

____

What are some ways that you can pause your thoughts?

____

____

____

____

____

How can you be more diligent when paying attention to details?

____

____

____

____

____

____

Discussion Notes, Thoughts, Prayers, and Additional Scriptures:

Discussion Notes, Thoughts, Prayers, and Additional Scriptures:

WEEK 10

Reading Relationships

Let's talk about relationships for a minute. Have you ever had one of those days where you're struggling in a relationship? Every single one of us has had those days, some of us a little less, some of us a little more. What about those days when you have a knockdown, drag-out, argument with your spouse, friend, parents, in-laws, and so on? The ones that leave you throwing your hands up in the air saying I can't do this anymore. The ones that make you feel unappreciated, where nobody sees your side of the story.

Guess what, we've all been there! Keep in mind, it's not if these events will happen. It's how we respond to them when they happen. One of my children was having a situation and struggled with feeling the pool of responsibilities between them and their spouse, a typical relationship issue. For example, if you think you were doing all the housework and your spouse is not carrying their weight, you may feel a little shafted. Maybe you are reorganizing your relationship instead of reestablishing it. The complex thing about relationships is it's usually based on more external perspectives than internal perspectives.

How do you know if you genuinely do all of the necessary items to keep the house running? Is it based on how much you're cleaning versus the other person, maybe based on how many errands you're running versus the other person? Could it be how much money one person brings in over the other? Would it be fair to say every piece of a relationship has an expense component and an income component?

You may not bring the financial aspects into your home. Maybe you do the diligence of the tasks you sow into your home's unity. You have to stop focusing on what someone brings to the table or what someone doesn't. Every relationship component has its variable that may or may not be beneficial to the whole relationship. If you've been at work all day to provide extra money for your family, come home, and your spouse has cleaned the house and made dinner, so all you have to do is relax the rest of the evening. Does that equate to monetary value? The answer is simple, yes! If you had to pay someone to complete those tasks, it would equal financial value as well as emotional and physical.

Most issues people tend to see in their relationships seem to be things like who is carrying the most weight or has the most invested. That happens in all aspects of relationships. Ultimately, it can lead to significant offenses.

For the vast majority of us, our desire for relationships has something to do with our fulfillment needs. This doesn't always mean that we're self-centered. It just means that we lack in some areas. There are so many avenues that lead us to be who we are. When we take the time to investigate our own needs and wants, we begin to see why we're dependent on others for our happiness. This isn't always a bad thing. However, you want to make sure you never overcompensate for something you lack to be fulfilled by someone else. God teaches us in His word that our worth comes from Him.

> *'Knowing that you were not redeemed with corruptible things, like silver or gold, from your aimless conduct received by tradition from your fathers, but with the precious blood of Christ, as of a lamb without blemish and without spot.' — I Peter 1:18-19 NKJV*

Many of us unknowingly want to parent our relationships. We have this need to help others see what we believe they can't. Unfortunately, when you are close to someone, that behavior gets amplified. Throughout this study, I have spoken of numerous relationships that I have had and the many ways God showed me how I and others' fears manipulated my relationships. The enemy is very cunning and knows how to destroy you if you let him. I have had many friendships over my lifetime. They have taught me that people can only see what they want and not the complete picture until God shows them true revelation.

If we would all take the time to view life through someone else's window, we may see things differently. Most never see how they hold you down. Most only can see what "they" are going through. Many may not have Grace for anyone other than themselves. Again, hurt people, hurt people. They want just as much deliverance as you do, but they may not know how to get it.

Forgive yourself first, and then forgiving others will start coming more naturally, whether they ask for it or not.

> *'Then Jesus said, "Father, forgive them, for they do not know what they do." And they divided His garments and cast lots.' — Luke 23:34 NKJV*

I can assure you there are always three perspectives to all situations. When we begin the self-reflection journey, we give ourselves an opportunity for growth. The only way we can obtain this is forgiveness in all avenues. Everything starts with self, from indulgent to corrections. Don't we all want to find the road of redemption? We have to start within before God can light the path for our future and others in our lives.

Maybe your struggle is finding friendship or love altogether. Perhaps you do not know how to read a situation. Could your vision be off because of fear of rejection or emotional damage? Life has so many twists and turns you may be missing your off-ramp to your perfect road.

During the years my husband was alive, he would say outrageous things. He loved to catch people off guard. He constantly told us one story: he would expect his best friend of eighteen years, Antoine, to take care of the kids and me if anything ever happened to him. Of course, we would all tell him he needed to stop talking like that because nothing would ever happen to him. We would joke that he was too ornery to die.

Besides that, I came from a family that did not believe in interracial relationships. Antoine was of a different race. My mother was not racist. Nonetheless, she was raised that the opposite race did not marry. Unfortunately, she grew up in an era that segregation was a real issue. I never understood it, and when asked, she never had a direct answer. Her response was always, "It's just the way I was raised." Many of her best friends were of a different race, so it always left me perplexed.

One day, as they like to refer to themselves, the two brothers from another mother had an in-depth conversation. For the first time, Antoine planned to get on that plane for Thanksgiving to meet his girlfriend's family. He thought he might want to propose. Kevin would laugh and laugh, saying, "You will never get on that plane." "Of course," Antoine would respond with, "I bought the ticket, and I am getting on the plane."

Antoine was one of the family. They even worked together off and on for many years. On November 23, 2015, Antoine was about to get on the plane, and my son called and told Antoine he had to come to the house that his dad had died and we needed him. Needless to say, he never stepped foot on that plane.

Well, the rest is a love story that will be left for eternity. I am very fortunate to have more than one love in a lifetime. You see, Antoine and I did get married a little over a year later. Our relationship was met with lots of speculation and obstinance. We could not make people less insensitive, but what we could do is make them less invited. No one had to love our story the way we did. However, they did need our account to help them change some of theirs.

The moments they didn't see were the testimony of ours. The sleepless nights when Antoine would allow me to lay my head on his chest and listen to the rhythm of his heartbeat, so I could fall asleep on the couch. The times when I would break down and could not breathe because of the pain from a broken heart, and he would embrace me with the love of a friend and a response of, "I miss him too." The moments where I was relieved the fighting was over, yet I felt guilty for having that emotion, and he understood. How about when my children were hurting and not being empathetic with me because of their pain? He would defend us all, never taking sides. The times the grass needed mowing or something needed to be repaired at the house. When I went somewhere I should not have, he had to go get me. Those were the moments they did not see—the moments where I started looking differently at him, more than a friend.

The great thing about God is He teaches us reading relationships is one of his most valuable gifts. First, it keeps us safe, but then it teaches us to love. God has big plans for us, and most of the time, we are so worried about what it will look like to others that we miss the greatest gift we could ever have on Earth. Don't deny people a relationship because of someone else's view.

Rejoice when God gives you what He knows you need, not when you obtain what you think you need. I had a list of my future. To be perfectly honest, Antoine was not on it. He did not line up with what I thought would work for my family. Then, God showed me my list wasn't His list. I would strongly advise you to lay down your thoughts and reach for our Father. He showed me what I needed, not what I wanted. Over time, my heart's desire changed in the way I looked at Antoine. I am glad that I read our relationship with the bifocals of God since my prescription was weak.

DATE: ____________________

Do you believe in your plan or God's?

____

How can you change your opinion of your relationships?

____

____

____

____

____

____

Are there ways that you can be more objective about the relationships in your life?

____

____

____

____

____

____

Discussion Notes, Thoughts, Prayers, and Additional Scriptures:

Discussion Notes, Thoughts, Prayers, and Additional Scriptures:

WEEK 11

God Loves You in Your Brokenness

The Lord is near to those who have a broken heart, And saves such as have a contrite spirit.
— Psalms 34:18 NKJV

Not so long ago, I decided to take the kids on a beach trip. Something I love to do, unfortunately, I don't get to do it very often. It's incredible how close you can live to a vacation spot and never get to utilize it. For us, we are thirty-five minutes from the beach. I think it is so tranquil, the salt air, the waves crashing, the sound of joy, and the fragrance of peace. That day the sun was bright, the sky was clear, and the water was relatively calm. I'd have to say the beach and the mountains are my favorite places on Earth. You can always see the artistic hand of God. Throughout both of those locations, they tell us a story without saying a word. They bring us the peace to endure the hardships of life. Yet, in the same breath, they bring us the restoration to conquer another day. The power of water is the power of one.

I'll never forget the lesson I learned from my stepson that day. People forget the greatest lessons usually come from those too innocent to understand the phrases of life. The ones that live in their innocence of love and no expectation of disappointment.

Children are the greatest gift of God, and yet we always discount the power they have. The Lord tells us to come to Him as children all the time, yet we think coming to him as a theologist will get us farther. When will we learn it's our innocence of love, the capability of kindness, and our strength of endurance that draws us much closer to God? More so than those things of arrogance, self-righteousness, and perfection. We speak to God as though we think He doesn't know our heart's desires. Oh, but He does.

As I'm sitting, looking out at the beautiful water, our child approaches me with a handful of shells. Now, unlike all of you, I was having a bad day. I was inundated with thoughts and struggles typical of life. I decided that as we were at the beach, I needed a lesson from God. When you wait for God to teach you a lesson, He always supplies a message.

> *'I love those who love me, And those who seek me diligently will find me.' — Proverbs 8:17 NKJV*

He opened up his hands and showed me lots of broken shells. In the sweetest, kindest voice, he stated, "Aren't they beautiful?" At that moment, I realized our perception of life is entirely inaccurate to the beauty God wants to show us. These shells to the average person would be thrown away. Truthfully, they would never have even had the opportunity to be picked up. They would be left to be walked upon. Just like in life, people tend to treat people just like that.

We want to pick up the beautiful shells, ones that have perfectly sculpted edges. The ones with surfaces of beautiful coloring. The shells that make the complete reflection of what we believe the definition of beauty is. The fact of the matter is, God sees beauty in our brokenness even when we can't hide. God wants us to open ourselves in transparency to Him with humility.

> *'For thus says the High and Lofty One Who inhabits eternity, whose name is Holy: "I dwell in the high and holy place, With him who has a contrite and humble spirit, To revive the spirit of the humble, And to revive*

the heart of the contrite ones.' — Isaiah 57:15 NKJV

The truth is he already knows everything. We can't hide any of our bruises or brokenness. God already knows that we would be broken. Even though, at first glance, they were broken shells. To God, they were beautiful. It takes the eyes of a child to see the fullness of God's beauty in the Earth.

You may be going through moments where you think no one sees your beauty because you're broken. You may think you're never going to be as good as someone else. I think we all have moments where we feel that we don't fit in. You don't fit in at church, you don't fit in the workplace, you don't even fit in your family, and then God sends us His message. The message that tells us we are good enough. He doesn't want us to be Frozen in Time with our insignificant view of who we think we are. Remember, fitting in is not your focus. God sets us apart at times for His glory.

You may not feel perfect now. I can assure you that you never will, which is ok. God is not after perfection. He is after obedience. Be willing to be groomed to the level that God has set for you. Break down your walls and let Him in. I am certain throughout this book you have seen the process. It is all about us having the vulnerability to talk with God. A journey that is to be traveled, one for transformation and not behavior modification.

God wants to be one with you. Not because you're after what he can give you because He is your Father and you are His child. Your creator designed you. He is not bothered by your imperfections. That is why He sent His Son, Jesus. Come, sit with Jesus behind the table. Prepare to be one of His disciples. I pray this journey catapults you to your God-given calling. Not the desires of yourself, the desires your Father has put inside of you.

May your brokenness be healed one moment at a time with your foundation being built on wholeness.

> *'Come to Me, all you who labor and are heavy laden, and I will give you rest. Take My yoke upon you and learn from Me, for I am gentle and lowly in heart, and you will find rest for your souls. For My yoke is easy and My burden is light.' — Matthew 11:28*

The Bible says we are to be like children. I know for us, that's quite a stretch. Most look at children and say they have very little to offer us in place of wisdom, but do they? I think children are the wisest creatures on the planet.

Have you ever noticed a child playing with another child and realized that when the child got frustrated, the next day, they went back and began playing together again? See, children don't hold judgment. We keep them as we become adults. Children give love that is seemingly so unconditional. Even in their hurts, they still want to love the broken.

Don't get me wrong, we must teach our children to be safe and guard their hearts. We also have to teach them that Christ wants us to love everyone, even our enemies. I genuinely believe the hurts we go through in our lifetime mold us into the adults we are. Then it takes God decades to undo us because we focus on the injuries that we've been through and not the pleasant events. God wants us to love everyone. It doesn't mean that you have to open the door and let everyone in. But it does mean you're supposed to give edification.

In 1 Corinthians 9:22, Paul talks about becoming what you need to become for others to help win them to Christ.

> *'For though I am free from all men, I have made myself a servant to all, that I might win the more; and to the Jews I became as a Jew, that I might win Jews; to those who are under the law, as under the law, that I might*

> *win those who are under the law; to those who are without law, as without law (not being without law toward God, but under law toward Christ), that I might win those who are without law; to the weak I became as weak, that I might win the weak. I have become all things to all men, that I might by all means save some. Now this I do for the gospel's sake, that I may be partaker of it with you.' — I Corinthians 9:19-23 NKJV*

It's what helps people grow. Improvement isn't based on how they treat you. It's based on the word of God. It's not an emotional circumstance; It's the behavior of Christ. I know for many, this is difficult since we've gotten wrapped up in a world of hurt. You may have heard that the world will never change, but we have God to help us create medicine that can cause the change.

Be grateful for the opportunities that God has shown us about our personalities. The ones that help us to be molded and refined like clay by the master. When someone is not kind to you, it is something within them that causes a disconnect. It is their brokenness. That just means that God is working on all of us one piece at a time. Don't let their brokenness define yours. When you think about a beautiful piece of pottery, it has to be moistened and softened into the shape God wants it to be. When it doesn't move to the correct form, he takes it back down to the beginning.

Children are multiplied by God, excited about learning. Children have granted the world innocence and happiness. Children are like plants; they grow when the sun shines upon them and soak up the rain when it falls on them. They grow where they're fertilized like a blooming fruit that is one of the sweetest delicacies. As you nurture them, they grow.

Right now, take a moment to think of children dancing and laughing and playing. Their laughter is contagious. It moves us to a happy place. That is what God wants for His creation. We are for His enjoyment, as I said earlier. God is waiting for us to revert to being children in the Kingdom. Those are the ones that are closest to Him. Not the ones that think they have it all figured out. He wants our innocence.

God already knows our hurts, but He is refining it to a place that won't leak the substance of pain. He is putting a seal on us that, when dropped, cannot be shattered. Let the potter's hand do what he's called to do. Let go of those pains and look at everyone as Christ does, keeping in mind to guard your heart. Nevertheless, give your love.

Make your Father proud! Be like a child, innocently open to His word.

> *'Behold what manner of love the Father has bestowed on us, that we should be called children of God! Therefore the world does not know us, because it did not know Him. Beloved, now we are children of God; and it has not yet been revealed what we shall be, but we know that when He is revealed, we shall be like Him, for we shall see Him as He is. And everyone who has this hope in Him purifies himself, just as He is pure.' — I John 3:1-3 NKJV*

DATE: ___________________________

Do you feel broken?

____

What things in your life sowed into your brokenness?

____

____

____

____

____

____

In what ways can you heal from your brokenness?

____

____

____

____

____

____

Discussion Notes, Thoughts, Prayers, and Additional Scriptures:

Discussion Notes, Thoughts, Prayers, and Additional Scriptures:

WEEK 12

Reconciliation and Restoration have No Deadline, NEITHER DOES YOUR TESTIMONY

Shortly after Kevin passed, Mom and I thought it best that we move in together. I needed a fresh start. I lost my home to foreclosure. Therefore, Mom and I agreed that I would make the payments on a new home, and she would do the financing for the loan. It was a big step for us. We were not sure how it would work because, half the time, we did not get along. However, she needed me, and I needed her.

I told Mom, Antoine and I would be getting married, and he would be living with us. She knew I loved him, and in her way, she knew this was God's direction for my life. The neat thing is she probably loves him more than me now.

We were all restarting our lives and learning to grow. We were also healing in the process. God knew what He was doing. Unfortunately, during that time, my daughter died. My poor mom had to repeatedly re-live this pain. What was worse was that she had to watch me hurt. No mother wants to see their children go through such heartache.

Within a year of Jess's passing, my mother was diagnosed with stage four small cell carcinoma. I realized finding my footing after a complicated time was more problematic than I knew. I remember saying to my husband, with tears flowing down my face, "I don't want to watch my mother die. I can't take this again." My mighty man of God looked me in the eyes and said, "Then watch her live."

With all problems come solutions. There was no way we were going to be moved by this. Do not get lost trying to find out why you are in something. Have the moment, just be. God reveals all things in His timing. He always unfolds the laundry when it is time to wear it.

I can't possibly know why we go through the obstacles we do. What I do know is that they don't define us. They may influence us, but they don't define us. As a child, I never thought my mom and I would ever have a relationship. God knew He would have the final say that would resemble the love of the Father. In the beginning, we struggle. However, as time evolves, so do God's people. Every barrier reroutes you to a passage.

If you had told me when I was in my twenties, my mom would change. I would never have believed you. Although I didn't wait for Mom to change, I made the change and hoped she would follow. Even if she didn't, I had a different relationship with God and had to be accountable for me, not her.

> *'For we do not wrestle against flesh and blood, but against principalities, against powers, against the rulers of the darkness of this age, against spiritual hosts of wickedness in the heavenly places. ' — Ephesians 6:12 NKJV*

God pursued me until I loved her with His love, the love that was unconditional and stable. It was an honoring love before she was sick. It allowed me not to question why I love her. I want to honor my mom, nothing more and nothing less.

> *'Children, obey your parents in the Lord, for this is right. "Honor your father and mother," which is the first commandment with promise: "that it may be well with you and you may live long on the earth."' — Ephesians 6:1-3 NKJV*

There are times when forgiveness occurs after a catastrophe. Then it leaves you questioning things like, "Am I doing this because of the situation they are in or because I have truly forgiven them?" Look, it doesn't matter if you reconciled before or after a life-altering event. What matters is that you resolve your issues. Once you obtain that, I believe you will have healing like no other.

God's love is not conditional, and neither should ours be. He doesn't care when it happens, He only cares that it happens. Stop hindering your growth by your pride. Let hurts that you are hanging onto be replaced with forgiveness. Again, forgive yourself, and then forgive others that hurt you.

Does freedom have a cost? Yes. That cost is you laying down everything you thought you knew, everything you imagined, and every pain you ever felt. If I had never let go of my pain where I would be today. I would have so much pride the fall would be inevitable. I hope the glimpse of my journey influences you to be a better you. One that will cause you to reflect on the hurts that you're holding. I believe we all have ups and downs. More extraordinary is that neither keeps us from our destiny. Whether your pain was gifted or formed, I hope you will leave it all at the cross.

Remember, the creative story of Christ increases with your testimony. There is no story Jesus hasn't seen. No triumph or discouragement he's not been a part of. Your testimony is your voice for God's word. We are to give an account for everything we do, just as Jesus gave an account for everything he did. We are to show the sacrificial change within us to the world. People can challenge so many things about you. What they cannot challenge is your testimony. It is your story and your story alone. It's the journey of Christ that you walked out with your Father.

Debates may happen over views, but testimonies cannot be debated. They are the real moments where time stood still and impacted your life. You must never forget to ask yourself what is the finale of your testimony. Is it one of great courage, strength, overcoming, and inward growth, or one of weakness, doubt, sadness, and outward fictional appearance? Christ gave us free will. We are the enablers of everything we walk out.

There are times in our lives where we will be weak, don't let that discourage you from your outcome. We are made of flesh and blood, and the Bible says we have to die to our flesh every day.

> *'Then He said to them all, "If anyone desires to come after Me, let him deny himself, and take up his cross daily, and follow Me.' — Luke 9:23 NKJV*

When you have those days that seem less than productive in Christ, leave it there that day. Tomorrow is a new day, a new strength.

Remember to tell the stories in your life where God did things. Tell the stories about your weak moments where God became your strength. Let your stories be such a testimony of the achievements of God that no one can debate you. People may never see what God sees in you to the fullest. They may get a glimpse of what God shows them, however, it will never be as great as God sees you.

God can look through the hopelessness that we have, he can look through the failures that we have, and he can look through everything that we have done that is not in accordance with righteousness. Man is not FULLY capable of that. Man sets us up for an expectation that he believes is the moral order of the Heavenly Father. Man doesn't always understand Grace. Grace is something that is given freely and not earned. It is provided to you with unconditional love.

Reflect on all the things that continue to grow you into the Christian God created you to be. Christ came for us all. None of us are more significant than the other; God is no respecter of people. Some people take longer to bear fruit than others. It does not mean that God loves them any less. It just means they're at a growth rate that differs from others. It does mean that you may not move in the fullness that God has for you until more fruit is born. Don't let that stop you from doing the work of the Kingdom. Let it cause you to reflect on the insufficient pieces of your walk.

> *'Then Peter opened his mouth and said: In truth I perceive that God shows no partiality.'*
> *— Acts 10:34 NKJV*

The Grace that God will give you, and in turn, He gives it to others. Love them where they are in their journey, with disliking their sin. Never say you don't like people. Just oppose their sin. You cannot dislike someone and, in the same breath, love them as Christ does. You can dislike their ways, not them as God's creations. Understand we are all working out our journey with individual substances.

> *'Brethren, if a man is overtaken in any trespass, you who are spiritual restore such a one in a spirit of gentleness, considering yourself lest you also be tempted. Bear one another's burdens, and so fulfill the law of Christ. For if anyone thinks himself to be something, when he is nothing, he deceives himself. But let each one examine his own work, and then he will have rejoicing in himself alone, and not in another. For each one shall bear his own load.'*
> *— Galatians 6:1-5 NKJV*

The primary law of Christ is love. Even the best Christians fall sometimes. When wanting to call out others, just be careful since that is a heart move. You may be correcting when God is not in the conversation. God says in His word we will all be judged. I am confident he has that covered.

I'm not saying that you cannot correct your brother and sister. I'm saying that God knows your heart, whether it is mere repetitiveness of word or true love and concern of God's people. They, too, have a testimony that will help the saved and unsaved alike. I pray that none of us will be so insistent on correcting others that we forget somewhere along the line their testimony may change someone. Please be conscientious of your intention. Never think you are higher than you are. Never believe that others are beneath you. Just like in the Bible, everyone has a story. Some of those stories have happy endings, and some don't.

Nonetheless, their walk is theirs, as well as their testimony, so always keep that in mind. I can genuinely say, thankfully, I allowed God to restore my relationship with my mother. I didn't get finalized in the hurt. Your testimony will be evangelized for many, and so will theirs.

Don't lose what God wants for you on the temporary road of life. Reconcile your worth, restore your hope, and keep in mind no one can dispute your testimony. Most importantly, God can move mountains; stop holding them in place.

> *'And they overcame him by the blood of the Lamb and by the word of their testimony, and they did not love their lives to the death. ' — Revelation 12:11 NKJV*

DATE: ______________________

Do you believe God can restore?

____

What in your past needs restoration?

____

____

____

____

____

____

How can God help restore you?

____

____

____

____

____

____

Discussion Notes, Thoughts, Prayers, and Additional Scriptures:

Discussion Notes, Thoughts, Prayers, and Additional Scriptures:

In Conclusion, I would like to personally thank you for your participation in my twelve-week Bible Study. I appreciate that you have walked with me through part of my own personal journey. More importantly, congratulations on your completion over these last weeks into your journey. I pray that you have been released from the moments where life held you in your prison. I know God has beautiful gifts for you, gifts that will forever change your life. I would love to hear how this study has transformed you in your unique path. Feel free to message me at any time and remember, "Only you can stop holding your mountains in place."

Works Cited

(2021, October 13). Retrieved from Bible: https://my.bible.com

2021 Online. (2021, October 13). Retrieved from Merriam Webster Online: https://www.merriam-webster.com/

James Strong, L. (1990). *The New Strong's Expanded Exhaustive Concordance of the Bible*. Nashville: Thomas Nelson Publishing.

The Holy Bible. (n.d.). Nashville: Thomas Nelson.

CPSIA information can be obtained
at www.ICGtesting.com
Printed in the USA
BVHW070011151221
624011BV00023B/1931